THROUGH THE MOUNTAINS AND THE STORMS

Melody Tilenis

WESTBOW
PRESS
A DIVISION OF THOMAS NELSON
& ZONDERVAN

WestBow Press books may be ordered through booksellers or by contacting:

WestBow Press
A Division of Thomas Nelson & Zondervan
1663 Liberty Drive
Bloomington, IN 47403
www.westbowpress.com
1 (866) 928-1240

ISBN: 978-1-4908-9036-4 (sc)
ISBN: 978-1-4908-9037-1 (e)

Print information available on the last page.

WestBow Press rev. date: 08/05/2015

Hope That You'll Hear

Trying to sleep
But these tears won't stop
Trying to live
But the lies won't end
Now I'm on my knees
Crying out to You
Hoping You'll hear
And take me back into Your arms

You'll Always Hold Me

Why does life seem so dark
Why do lies seem to haunt me
Torturing me each day
Until I cry out to You
Until I realize holding onto You
Is what will get me through

Laying In Silence

As the breeze sways the grass
With eyes closed as I listen
For Your heartbeat and Your voice
God, come close so You can whisper to me
Whisper that You love me
Let me know that You're there
And that You know me better
Than anyone ever will

Save Me From Myself

Knowing now that I need You here
I need You to walk with me
Through my darkest hours
I need You to pull me out
Of the crashing waves
And save me from this raging storm
That I call my hell

Lesson In Silence

Teach me to be still
Hold me close for just one second
As I learn to sit silently with a thoughtless mind
And a quiet mouth
Hold me near You
As You speak to me
As You whisper to my soul

Jesus Break Through

Shine Your light into my heart

Tear down the walls that surround it

Let Your love break through

And pull me up out of the hole

I have again fallen into

Be my retreat for when the world attacks

Be my rock that I can hide under

Show me how to live again

And escape into only You

I need to be all I can be

But I need You to guide me

So shine Your light back into the dark

Help me open up my heart once again

And reveal to me what it means to follow You, Jesus

How Great You Are

God, You're my God
You know me and all my thoughts
Forever I need You by my side
Lord, You hold me and You guide me
You are the rock I can hide under
You're my shelter when it storms
And You're always with me
You love me as Your bride
And with love like a Father as Your child
I will forever give You thanks
For how great You are

Beauty in the Darkness

The blue sky above me
The green grass under my feet
The flowers sway as Your glory is revealed
The birds sing Your praises
So this is how creation loves You
When the sun burns bright
And the moon glows in the darkness
I can hear the crickets singing
And feel the stillness of the night
As it displays Your beauty

Light in the Heavens

Darkness
I try to run
I try to scream but it closes in fast
Faster than these walls that close in
Then I look up
I see that You're above me
Your light shining through
Your hand reaching out
To pull me out of the enclosed room
Yet I always run back
To these lies in my mind
That seem to hold me down
To the secrets that haunt me
That I never let go of
But when I look up, they are revealed
I tremble with fear
As I turn my face upward

I Could, I Might

I could dance on top of the world

But then I might lose control

I could stare at you forever

But then your life might flash before my eyes

I could love you for all eternity

But then my hopes might come crashing down

I could sit here pretending everything is OK

But then my tears might flood the earth

Or I could quietly listen to Him

While He holds me in His arms

Slowly Saving Me

Screaming

I'm screaming for You to save me

Bleeding

In a different time and land You're bleeding for me

Knowing

You know I need You to save me

Trying

You're trying to break through this wall around my heart

Crying

I'm crying as I slowly give into Your love

Holding

I'm trying to live this life holding onto You every step I take

Your Love & Your Peace

I breathe in
And as I let it out
I close my eyes
Just to let You whisper to me
You speak calmly to my heart
While You hold me in Your arms
You tell me that You love me
And as the pain fades
You fill me with Your peace

The Hour, The Day, The Moment

Waiting for the day
When I'll be by Your side
When I hear You say
That You've always loved me
Waiting for the moment
When I'll be in Your arms
When You'll be the only One
That I know I've always needed
Waiting for the hour
When You call my name
When I'll be with You
And in Your loving presence
Forever and for all eternity

Lonely, Darkened Land

Crying out to You
From in this darkened land again
With this broken heart
I need Your love
To come down and surround me
And Your touch
To repair the brokenness
To stop the bleeding

Why You Care

How do You stand me
When there are days I can't stand You
What makes You love me
When I feel unloving towards You
Why do You take me back
Even after I mess up again
Why do You run to me
When I run from You

Breathing in Your Air

I wanna be Yours

I wanna live loud

Louder than I ever have before

I wanna run to Your arms

And cry on Your shoulder

I wanna breathe in Your air

And drown in Your water

But most of all I want to fall

Fall more in love with You

Falling Into You

I'm ready and I'm willing
But I still need Your help
To get through the days
The earth throws at me
I need You to hold me close
As I walk through this life
I need You to help me back up
If I ever fall back down
And I need You to be first
No matter what happens
Or who has come into my life

Drifting Into You

Close my eyes
Breathe into me
Hold onto me
As I drift away
I need to reach out to You
I need Your arms around me
Please send Your light to help me
To heal my hurting soul
And to mend my broken heart
Let me call to You
In these last hours
And when it's all over
Take me up to my true home

Into My Arms

I'll take your hand
And pull you out
Of the darkness
Out of the dirt
I'll give you new eyes
To see My light shine
And I'll wash you clean
To where you're white as snow
I'll set you free
From the chains that held you down
I'll pick you up into My arms
And hold you close while you cry
I'll laugh when you laugh
And I'll love you with more love
Than anyone can ever give

Everything that I Am

I am your calm

I am your peace

I am love

I am your strength

I am your hope

I will lift you up when you fall down

I am your shelter in the storm

I am your life

I am your Father

I will listen when you cry

I Am

Who You Are In Me

"Lean in close"
You whisper to my heart
"I will tell you the truth.
You are beautiful
You are loved
You are smart
You are My child
And I will never let you go
I hold you in My arms
And I am with you always
You are free from the chains
That once held you down
Because you believe
I will guide you back home
To the place you belong
Because you trust Me
I love you and will never let you go

Knowing You'll Save Me

Where is this going
How did I fall
Into the sea of loneliness
And the ocean of a broken heart
Now that I'm drowning
I see that You're above
Reaching down so I will reach up
So You can pull me back
Back up into the heavens
And into Your arms
Where I will be safe
And where You'll heal my heart

My Light and My Breath

When darkness closes in
Will there still be light
When things turn to disaster
Will hope still heal my soul
You are my light in this black night
You are my hope in this hell
When I feel like I can't breathe
Will air still fill my lungs
When I feel like giving up
Will You still hang on
You are the breath that fills my lungs
You are the hand that holds on
When the whole world is freezing
Will my heart still feel warmth
You are the blanket that covers my soul
You are always there and will never change

Falling Another Day

Crashing again
Spinning within
Trying to hold on
With everything that's in me
And needing to see
The light at the end
When You're the one who will win

Fortress and Salvation

My God, You are my fortress

The ground that I stand on

The mountain I go to

When the flood waters rise

My shelter when it storms

You are the peace that pierces through my fear

You are the love that kills the hate

You are the Light in the darkness

And You will take my pain

And turn it into hope and joy again

These Things to Remember

I'm slipping away, spiraling downward
And now I am screaming
When are You coming?
You tell me "Do not forget
That it is I who made you
Who loves you and will never let go"
So now I am on my knees
Begging for Your help
And for You to come close

Restoration of the Broken

Trying to fight through lies
And get out of my mind
God, I need You, I need Your strength
I need Your love and peace
So I can make it through the fire
That blocks me away
Away from what's real
And away from You
Help me to see You again
And to make it through these doubts

Like Breathing Without Air

I disappeared into the unknown
I ran so far from You
Then I realized
I can't do life without You
Like I can't breathe without air
So I searched for You
And You found me and brought me back
Back to the familiar place
Of Your loving arms and calming voice

Searching For My Lost and Broken Heart

Will You leave Your place
To find me wandering in the dark
Where I've been searching
For arms to hold me close
Would You search these white grains of sand
To find the darkened one
And turn it back again
Would You reach down
To find my lost heart
And to hold it close to You again
Will You send Your love to me
When I'm searching through all the hate
Would You pick all my tears up
As they fall to the ground
And then come close
Just so You can hold me
So I can feel Your heartbeat
And hear You whisper in my ear

Shouting Louder, Dreaming Higher

You thought you could drag me down
But He pulled me higher than before
You thought you could destroy my heart
But He restored it with His unfailing love
You thought you could silence my voice
But He spoke truth to me, even in my chaos
You thought you could darken my life
But He shone His light into my empty soul

My Questions, His Answers

In the silence of the night
When faith seems dead
Are You there to hold me in Your arms?
When darkness seems to overtake me
And I am crying out to You from my heart
Are You listening?
When the tears will not stop falling
Are You there to wipe them away?
When the hurricane winds
Are blowing in my mind
Will You calm the storm
With Your voice?
As I lay still I hear You whisper

"My child
Nothing will ever steal your faith
I see your heart, and know you believe
I hold you in My arms and will never let you go
I shine My light into your darkness
And I hear your prayer
And the cry of your heart
I will wipe your tears away
And will let you cry on My shoulder
I will speak one word
And calm the storm and give you peace
I love you more than you will ever know"

Written Death, Written Life

Before my life started
It was written in death
I was searching
Not knowing which direction I was in
But then it all turned around
I found Him with His arms open
Calling for me to come
Now it's all written in life

Leaving Me Behind

I tried to find you
But you were nowhere near your home
I tried to keep you at the center
But you kept moving throughout the crowd
Now I'm pushing my way through people
That never seem to matter to me
Just to be the center of your attention

As The Ice Breaks

The ice breaks
I sink into this freezing water
I struggle to gain air
As my hands flail through the water
Needing to find something, anything to grasp
You're reaching out, trying to grab my hand
Yet I can't see or feel you
Now I'm wondering if I'll ever get out
If I'll ever be the same
Or if I'll ever find warmth in your arms

This Fire That Burns

These flames
They climb higher
They crawl up the walls
This smoke
It chokes me
It blinds me until I cannot see
The path in front of me
My world
It caves in around me
Crashing down
Until there is nothing left standing
These walls that once were
Are no longer able
To hold in my pain
To shut everyone out
I try to build them back up
But as I pick up the bricks
They crumble to dust
And slip through my fingers

Waiting

Will the wait ever end?
Will I ever love
Only to be loved back?
Will I ever hold the one in my arms
While he holds me back?
It feels like
I'm always lying awake
Crying for someone
To be there with me
And for this wait to end

Ignoring The Inside

Can you even hear me?
As I cry out
Because of the pain and hurt
That's eating away my insides
Slowly tormenting me
Can you even hear me?
While I lay here
Wide awake at night
Trying to hold back tears
So my pillow doesn't get wet
Can you even hear?
Because it feels like you've abandoned me
And left me alone
So I have no one to run to

Danger Around

Freezing ice
With fire around
I'm standing in the middle
Knowing I'll sink
But unsure when
As it cracks
The fire gets higher
There's no way to escape
As I go under
I scream for help
Before icy water
Clogs up my lungs

Under These Stars

Under the stars
I know there's a greater hope
A greater love that I've felt
Many times before
As I stand here
With my face upward
And my eyes closed
The wind rushing through my hair
I sense you coming towards me
And as your love surrounds me
I know that you have always been
And will always be with me

To Bleed For Me

Sometimes I fall
Sometimes I doubt
But one thing that never falters
Is your love for me
It gets so hard to believe
That you'd be willing to bleed for me
That you'd want to take the beatings
That I deserve but don't get
How can you tell me you love me
When I should be hated
How can you stand to hold me
When I've done so many things wrong

Untitled

Is it possible

That love can be hated

Is it possible

That eyes that see can be blind

Is it possible

That broken hearts

Will somehow be healed

Is there a light in the dark

It seems right now

That I can hate love

That I cannot see

And my heart is breaking

But I don't see any light

With the darkness that overtakes me

Calling To You

If I call Your name
Will You come down?
If I reach for Your hand
Will You reach back
And pull me up out of the hole
The hole that I call my hell?
Will You save me when I'm drowning?
Will You send Your angels
To the flare that I send up?
Because I'm sending out the flare
Hoping that You'll see
And pick me up right now
Out of the mud I'm sinking in

Life In The Red Letters

I found life
In the pages of a book
As I read the black letters
I saw all the hate
When I closed my eyes
I saw the words I spoke
Beating Him as the lies seeped out
And tormenting me
I found love
Between the red letters
When I opened my eyes
He was kneeling there
Praying for me
Where the roses and lilies grew
And the trees stretched to the sky
Then He stood up
He held out His arms
Waiting for me to run to Him

Repeated Disasters, Repeated Returns

Bring me back to You

Even if it has to be slow

Re-ignite the passion

And the flame that once burned bright

Hold me tighter in Your arms

And don't let me go

Awaken me in the morning

And sing me to sleep at night

Don't let me fall away

And don't let me drown

God I am crying out to You

For You to save me again!

Chained and unfeeling

How can I be free
When I'm chained on the inside
How can I know the truth
When there are lies all around
I try to listen for Your voice
But the voices keep screaming
I try to open my eyes
But there's a shadow of doubt
Now I'm crying out
For you to rescue me from the fear

Hurting Obsession

How long?
How long do I live this way
With a hurting and broken heart
Each day gets harder
Every minute brings pain
How can I live
And still be dead inside
Loneliness eats at me
And it tears me apart
Will I ever feel love?
Will I ever feel You?
Will I ever find the Light again
Obsession brings damage
And fear brings darkness
I know I need You
But it's hard to want You
With tears clouding my eyes
And smoke all around
How will I ever see the sun again?

Why

Why are you running
From the One who keeps you safe
Why are you lying
About all the things you once knew as Truth
Why are you crying
When I'm trying to dry your tears
Why are you fighting
The only arms that hold you
And the whisper of love that surrounds you

To Understand Again

Take me back to the place I belong
Help me remember the familiar arms
The arms that once held me
And kept me from danger
And the love that once guarded me
Show me who You are again
Show me what is real
Help me understand again
Teach me how to see Your Light
And how to look into Your eyes
And hear You saying "you belong to Me"

Restore Your Vision

How can you see
When your vision is distorted
How can you believe
When what you believe in
Will only let you down
You say you know love
Yet your heart is still hurting
But I know of One
Who will hold you always
Who will tell you He loves you
And never let you go
His name is Jesus
He can heal your bleeding heart
And restore your broken soul
He can give you peace
When the fear closes in
He will be there always

Taking Me Down

Are You able to hold me
When the world is crashing down?
Are You able to see through all the lies
That spin around in my mind
Making these webs of doubt grow stronger
Are You able to shine Your light
Through the darkened fear
That haunts me in the night?
And will You fight for me
When my strength is all but gone
And hope has lost its place

Calming My Fear

I cry to a blank wall
As fear slowly creeps in
The darkness overwhelms me
And I cannot breathe
Just when I'm about to let go
You reach down and pick me up
Out of the overwhelming blackness
And gripping paranoia
You take me to a place of Your love
And into Your calming light
You give me peace I can't explain
And set me back down gently
With a new courage in my heart

Light Into My Soul

These dark walls stand so high
Building up higher with every fading hope
I hide myself away from You
Thinking I can never measure up
Just when I feel I'm about to let go
You break through the walls I've built up
You tear through the lies
That have destroyed me for so long
Leaving me a hopeless mess of despair
You restore my vision
And bring light back into my soul
You hold me closer than ever before
And promise me that You will never let go

What Can Defeat All Fear

Fear
It can eat at your soul
Grip you so tight
It won't let you go
It will choke you
Strangle you until there's nothing left
But I know of the very One that will defeat fear
He brings Light into the darkness
And penetrates it until there's nothing left to fear
His Name is Jesus
And He holds the victory

A Lie Hidden Inside

Pretty girl
With pain in her eyes
The lies she hides
On the inside
That run circles in her mind
The scars she covers
As she gets older
Never seem to fade
How can you look
Straight into her soul
And not see the hurt
That torments her
Eats her alive each night
And won't let her go

Addicted Chemical

You're my chemical
So intoxicating
Yet burning on the inside
You penetrate my heart
And deep into my soul
I'm so addicted
And yet so afraid
I try to let go
But I still hang on
Does anybody see
The fear that leaves me paralyzed
On the inside

Drowning in Doubt

I'm screaming
Grasping for love
I'm drowning
In this sea of doubt
And the lies that pull me under
Will not let me go
I'm choking on the words
That have told me I'm worthless
I'm fighting for a life
That seems all but hopeless
How can I ever return
When the vines of torment
Drag me down and entangle me
How can I jump
When there are no arms to hold me

Fighting Rising Water

Who will hold me
When the world goes dark
And I cannot see a light
That would guide me home
Who will reach for me
When the water is rising
And I cannot catch my breath
Will You be there to lift me up
If I fall and can't walk
Will You be by my side
As I am fighting all the lies
That hold me back
And out of Your arms

Spinning World

My world starts spinning
Every time you come close
Do you see what I go through
When you are near me
My heart beats faster
When you say my name
What do you see
When you look into my eyes
Can you tell that I lose myself
And am at a loss for words
When you are close

To Believe Again

I want to believe again
I want to remember
How Your love for me
Would consume me
How You'd hold me
And whisper in my ear
How You'd take my hand
And guide me back to You
I need You and Your peace
I need to love You
Like a little girl loves her daddy

Defeating the Darkness

When the shadows move in
And darkness tries to hide the light
You'll be there to guide me through
To hold my hand and whisper truth
You'll send Your armies
To fight the despair
And protect me from lies
That would try to drag me down
You'll wake me with Your calming voice
And in the morning I will seek You
As You pour out Your love on me
Along with the sunlight

Shadows in the Night

These shadows that chase me
Haunt me in the night
Trying to drag me away
From all that is safe
I cling to Your hand
And beg You not to leave
As the shadows try to tempt me
Away from Your love

Guiding Me Home

Jesus, take this life
Take my hand
Lead me to what is true
Show me the path
That You would want me to take
And guide me home if I'm ever lost
Hold me in Your arms
And wipe away the tears
If they should ever start to fall
Give me peace that no world can give
And love that no human could imagine
Shine Your light into the darkest shadows
And pick me up if I fall down

Facing You

Do you see the fear
That I feel when you come close
Can you sense all the emotions
That I fight to control
When I see you here
I call to the One
Who will strengthen me
I cry out to the Giver
Of the peace I need
To face you and set me free
From all the feelings
That torment me when you're near
He is my rock
My steady shelter
When the waves crash around
He is what I need
With Him, I will get through

Not A Slave

I'm not a slave to sin
I belong to God
He holds my future in His hands
And He will never fail me
He will listen when I call
And will pick me up if I stumble
He forgives, and He loves me
Enough to correct me when I'm wrong
I go to Him when things get crazy
He is what I need

Everything

You're my everything
You know me more
Than I could ever know myself
You hold my life in Your hands
You always know what's best
Even when I don't
You go before me
And You are behind
When I've fallen down
You lift me up
And back into Your arms
Your love is stronger
And better than any love
A human could ever give

Releasing You

Releasing all the pain
That I've been holding inside
Letting go of you
So I can live again
I need to breathe
And learn to live
Without you by my side
To be with the One
Who is my only comfort
Who is my only shelter
In the pain and the storm
Because I'm slowly realizing
That you can't be my everything
Only Jesus can love me
The way I need

In My Mind

In my mind, you're always with me
In my mind, you're holding me close
In my mind, our happier moments never end
In my mind, you always seem to know what I need
And you love me like I need

Letting Go All Control

I need to let go
And give You all things
That I try to control
Help me seek You
Let me find You
Show me what true love is
Show me Your peace
Take my hand
And guide me to Your truth
Show me the hope
Of the future
That I have in You
I need to lay my life
And all I have, all I want
At Your feet and give You
Complete control

Drowning In Fear

Save me
Once again I'm drowning
Pull me out of the torture
That I got myself into
Help me get out
Of the hole of fear
That I've dug my way into
These doubts and this worry
Plague my mind
The voices speak
And try to convince me
That I'm nothing in Your eyes
Remind me that I'm worth it
And that You alone can save me
From all the lies that drag me down

I Am

I Am your calm
I Am your peace
When you call on me
I Am your joy
Your shelter in the storm
I Am all you need
I Am love
And the truth that sets you free
I Am with you always
And will catch you when you fall
I Am grace
I Am forgiveness
I Am the one who will guide you home
When it is too dark to see

Chased Down Again

These demons are chasing me
Trying to drag me down again
As I try to hold onto hope
They throw their lies
Around in my mind
As they try to chain me down
I cry out for the only One
I know will rescue me
I reach out to the only Hand
That will pull me up if I fall

To Feel Again

I want to hope again
I want to feel
I want to be alive
These dreams that have died
Can they ever live again?
Are You still there
When I cry out
Do You still love me
Even when I mess up
Will You silence the voices
That have whispered their lies
That have kept me from living
And stolen away the peace
I still need You

Even when I scream that I don't
My soul longs for You
Even with the darkness closing in
I don't want to die here
I need You to remind me
Of the future I have in You
I need to know
That You will take me back
No matter how far I fall
No matter what I've said
No matter what I've done

Calling Out For You

Why are you running
From these arms of love
Why are you trying to hide
When you can never be hidden
I'm calling to you
For you to come back
I'm reaching out to you
So you won't fall further
Yet you still run
You still try to hide
From the only love
That can rescue you

Listen For His Voice

You're lying here
Hoping someone will save you
I'm reaching out for you
But you don't seem to see
These arms of love
That are waiting to save you
I'm calling for you
But you won't open up and listen
For My still, small voice
That would calm your racing heart
And ease all your fear
You need Me
Even though you won't admit it
And I want you to see
All the hope of a future
That I have for you
If you'll just run to Me

Shelter in the Storm

Jesus, my rock and salvation

My shelter from the raging storm

Thank You for Your mercy

And Your forgiveness

Teach me how to trust You

Even through the hard times

With everything and not just one thing

You are LORD, and I will bow down

Now and in the end before You

I need You, now help me to want You

Help me love You

And show me Your love for me

Wash Away Lies

The desire of death
Comes along with the lies
That I'm not pretty enough
Not smart enough
Not good enough for anyone
I call out to You
Hoping You'll wash away
All the lies and remind me
That death has lost its sting
That I am beautiful in Your eyes
And that's all that should matter

Closing in Again

My walls are closing in
Can You save me?
These tears they will not dry
Can You hear me?
I'm crying out
Desperate for a whisper
A touch, anything to set me free
Somewhere in my mind
In my heart, in my soul
I know I need You
To rescue me and pull me through
Will You show me hope again?
Show me what Your love is like again
Will You reach out Your hand
And pull me out of this darkness
Away from these lies
That are tearing me apart

Ocean Depths

This ocean swallows me
Drifting me away
Into the depths below
Now I'm crying out Your Name
Grasping for something
That will pull me out of the sea
You reach out Your hand
And rescue me from the raging waters
You pull me into Your ship
And into safety again

Soaring like an Eagle

Waves crash against the shore
The mountains rising into the sky
I stand in awe of all You've made
An eagle takes flight
I spread my arms
And let the wind take me away
To a place with You
I let Your breath fill my lungs
As I breathe in
This is what it's like to feel alive
To know You are with me
Every second, every day

Chasing Me, Calling for Me

I am running from You
Trying so hard to find my own way
As I run, You run too
Chasing me down, calling for me
Knowing I will hear
And someday soon
I will turn back
And run straight into Your arms again

Calling Me to You

My heart searches for You
My soul longs for You
As I wander through this desert
I look for You
I long for Your living water
Your bread to fill me up
I desperately still need You
I hear You calling me
Awakening me slowly
From the sleep I fell into
As You shine Your light
Into my world, I grasp for You
Needing Your breath in my lungs again

A Dream Broken

I had a dream
That I was lost and broken
Searching for a hand to hold
Or a soul to save me
You were in front of me
Right there holding out Your arms
Calling for me to come back
But I still ran
Looking, searching for someone
Will this search ever end?
Will I ever realize
That You are right here
Waiting for me, calling for me
Somehow I know
In my mind somewhere
That I still need You
But still I keep on running
And I keep searching

Leading Me to Your Love

Hold me, hold me in Your arms
Never let me go
Show me, show me all Your love
Help me overcome this fear
That holds me down
And chokes me up
I want to stand for You
And even if they try to shut me up
I want to be louder than before
And tell the world about who You are
You alone deserve all the glory
And honor this world could ever offer
You are the light in the darkest nights
Leading me into Your presence
You are the perfect love
That casts out all my fears
And all my sorrows
So show the world who You are
And what You can do through my life

More to Life

We could be dreamers

Unbroken, unbound

Chains would no longer hold us down

We could reach for the stars

And grab life in our hands

We could dive into the sea

Free, wild

Loving would be easy

And we would lose no more

Our hopes could soar

With nothing to crush them down

We could be free to dance

Through the endless sky

But here we are

With a weight to tie us down

As we look up and wish

For a life of more

No Looking Back

Don't look back
Don't look down
Move forward
Away from the past
Away from the lies
That haunt you day and night
There is a light
At the end
And when you reach it
The tears will be gone
The pain will fade
You'll feel love
As you've never felt it before
Happiness and joy will be there
For all eternity
But keep pressing on
Hang on a little longer
And He will guide you there
If you let Him

Forgetting, Remembering

My world spins every time
Every time you come around
It's something that I hate
But something that I like
I want to escape you
But I also want you close
You make me happy
And that makes me mad
How can I let go
When I want to keep hanging on
I think of you at night
And at sunrise I try to forget
All the dreams I had of you
Sometimes I can stand you
And sometimes I don't want you near
It's a battle to forget
And also to remember
I wonder which will win
And if it can ever end

Whole World Watching

You were never supposed to find me here
With the whole world watching
As you exposed me for who I really am
Looking past the lies, past all the hate
You tore me open, broke me down
You took who I was, who I am
And turned it into a whole new me
You created me to be who you needed
Who you wanted to use
You shook me up, and never let me stand still
You kept me moving into this new direction
You left me wanting, needing more of you
You kept me searching as I wandered
Through the desert and through the dark
Searching for water in this land
A light in the night
Something to guide me back home
Back into His waiting arms

Untitled

You've been there
To watch me grow
You've been there
To see me smile
To see me laugh
And sometimes cry
We've shared many things
And we've shared many moments
Now I'm saying thank you
For all the things you've done

Out of Darkness

Bring me back
To what I once believed
Show me the love that You give
And set me free
From the chains that hold me down
From the doubt that floods my mind
Take my hand and guide me
Out of the darkness that swallowed me
And back into Your light

Singing I am Free

You said that I am free
So I will shout that I am free
You said that I am loved
So I will sing of Your love
You said that I am beautiful
So I will dance for You
You said that I am Yours
So I will live knowing You are mine

Hope in Your Arms

You are my shelter
You hold me in Your arms
You will keep me safe
You are my hope when I feel hopeless
You will be my strength when I feel weak
When I need love You will love me
When I feel lonely You will come close
I call out to You knowing You will hear

Hoping You're Out There

Sometimes it seems as though we'll never meet

It gets hard to hold onto

The hope that you're out there

That you're waiting for me

It hurts to see these people in love

When I'm feeling so alone

Alone in this world, and in this life

Wordless Hopes

Trying to scream things
My mouth forming the words
Yet what I say makes no sense
What I do has no meaning
So I just lie here
Hoping someone will understand
And pull me up from the ground
Where I'm screaming wordless hopes

Near Me and With Me

I need You
You're like my drugs
I need You in me
You're like oxygen in my lungs
I need You near me
You're like the breeze against my skin
I need You with me
You're like the water I drink

You Can Hear, You Can Heal

My God, You can heal me

My God, You can hear me

When I cry out

You hold me in Your arms

You give me strength to make it through

As I sleep in darkness

I dream of Your light

Understanding Me

As I lie here
I feel Your arms
As they hold me tight
God, You never let me go
You hold my heart
And as I cry out to You
You listen and You understand
You are there in the shadows
And You hold the whole universe
I see You in the beauty of nature
And though I am small
You still care enough to come to me

Glimpses of Truth and You

Caught in between
Of the wanting and needing
Not knowing a safe way out
All directions seem to pull me in
Unsure of which to choose
I go up through the sky
And into the unknown
Hoping that You'll meet me there
And guide me with Your light
So if I fall again into my hell
There will always be a glimpse of hope
That drags me back out
And into Your loving arms

Holding Me Near You

Will You hear me
When I call out to You
As thoughts plague my mind
Will You hold me
When I lie on my bed
Shaking as tears run down my face
I want to believe
That You can save me
But sometimes it gets so hard
To run to You
When all I feel like doing
Is giving up and dying
You're the One who will heal me
Whenever my heart is breaking
You're the One who will fill me
If I ever feel empty inside
And You're the Light for my soul
Whenever darkness starts to creep in

Your Love Surrounds Me

I forget so much
That You're always with me
That Your love is better
Than what a human could give
Will You help me see
And remind me when I need it
That You surround me
In the darkness or in the light
That You'll always love me more
No matter who I meet
And no matter where I go

Untrue Dreams, Unanswered Hopes

These days are slowly fading
And as they turn to night
I look to the sky and wonder
How long before these tears dry
When will my daydreams and hopes
Become real and true
When will my prayers
Turn into something more

Uncertain Hope

My heart pours out
Through these words
Onto blank pages
From the inside of my soul
I sing through this pain
That keeps me awake at night
Trying to trust in someone unseen
And unsure of what tomorrow may hold

Untitled

I am down on my knees, face to the floor
Wondering if You hear, hoping that You will
I need You with me, I need Your love
I need to be in Your loving arms again
Protected and far away from danger
Far from the enemies arrows
That have rained down on my soul
For far too long

Restored Beauty

Staring
As a rose withers and dies
Its petals fallen on the ground
Feeling
My hopeless heart beats
With pain held inside my chest
Speaking
I am here, calling to You
Needing You to save me
Watching
As You pick the petals up
And restore it to beauty again
Letting go
As You give hope to my heart
And help it beat painlessly
Quiet and still
You hush me with Your calm voice
As You wrap Your strong, loving arms around me

Wishing For You

With every time my heart beats
The pain of losing you gets stronger
And the peace I once felt
Turns into hopelessness
Where did the dream go
The dream of us being together
When did this hope of you and me
Fade into the torture that eats my soul
That rips at my heart
To where I cry out every night

Screaming Through the Pain

I'm screaming out "where are you now?"
I'm lying here feeling faded and torn
Trying to remember and look for Your promises
As the tears start to fall
You take my hand and whisper in my ear
"You're not alone."
And when the fear creeps in
And doubts start to swirl
You gently tell me
"Do not be afraid, I am with you even now."
So I will trust and run into Your arms
And remember that You will never leave me
Even in the joy

Rewinding and Restarting

Motionless I lay here
Have these tears run their course?
I'd love to rewind
And start over without this
I cry to You night and day
Hoping for some way of escape
But now I've given up
Is it too late to return?
Or am I stuck in this hole?
Jesus, please rescue me
And pull me up
Up to a place of refuge
And into Your arms

Peace in the Fear

Fear overtakes me
As I approach the crowd
I start to tremble
And it seems I can't stop
I cry to You on the inside
"Jesus, help me!"
Slowly I feel Your peace
Start to fill my heart
And You remind me
I am not alone

Emptiness Filled

You build me up
When I am torn down
You heal me
When I hurt
You fill me up
When I am empty
You are my warmth
When I am cold
You hold me in Your arms
When I feel like letting go
You put me back together
When I've fallen apart

Needing Your Rescue

I need to breathe again
I need to see
I need Your voice
And I need Your touch
Can You rescue me
From this darkness I've slipped into?
Can You pick me up
From where I've fallen?
Will You hold out Your hand
And guide me back to You?
I'm screaming again
And hoping You'll hear
Because I'm at the end of myself
And holding onto a faded hope

To Come Back to Your Love

When did my heart stop beating

When did I run away

From the loving arms that held me

From all the truth that could set me free

I can hear You screaming

"Come back! Come back! Don't run any longer."

But still I escape You

And try to do things my way

When will I learn

From all the mistakes that have hurt

When will I see

The only love that will never die

Running to My Father

How could I run
From a love that's better
How could I hide
From the One who created me
He said He had a plan
He told me Truth
Yet still I disappeared
Into the driest desert
Now I'm looking for water
In a black land
I'm looking for Truth
In a world full of lies
I get on my knees
As I cry out to the Forgiver
And the Savior of my soul

Restoring Love

Restore my hope, restore my vision

Bring Light into the dark places

Take the stone that is my heart

And open it up to You again

Speak to me and love me like no other

Tell me Truth that will kill the lies

Hold me in Your arms and don't let me go

Whisper that You love me

And will never leave me

Pull my focus back to You

I need You, God

I need Your touch

Don't Let Go

Save me
Hear me
Rescue me from falling
Reach down and hold onto me
Pick me up again and don't let me go
I need You to love me
And don't ever stop
I need You to hold me
And let me cry into Your chest
Erase my past, erase my sin
Tell me I'm beautiful
And help me believe it
Because now letting go feels right
So please whisper to me
Tell me "Hold on, I'm with you
I'm with you in the dark
I'm with you in the pain
I will help you fight through the fear
That holds you back
I will give you rest
Just call on me and I will be there."

Slipping Into my Mind

Save me from drowning
From sinking into my mind
Hold my hand, guide me
Back to where You are
I need You, I need Your love
I need Your peace and Your truth
To break these chains
That slip around my ankles
And trip me as I try to walk

Screaming for my Savior

I'm screaming for You, my Savior
Untie these ropes that choke me
Shine Your light of Truth
And break through the lies
They are holding me down
And I can't escape
As they wrap me up
And tear me apart

Falling Further Into Darkness

Dark Places
Hurting faces
They all blend into one
I search for light
I grasp for a hand
Anything to guide me home
But everywhere I search
Everything I grasp
Pulls me further into darkness
And further away from You
Now I'm screaming
Searching for a way out
Of the hole and fear that I've fallen into

Never Stop Chasing Us

You'll never stop chasing me
If I run away, You'll come too
You reach out Your hand
And catch me when I fall
You love me
Even when it's hard to love You
You find me if I'm lost
You'll light up the night
And the dark places of my heart
You want me
When it's hard to want You
You know I need You
When I'm straying away

Slowly Awakening

I'm slowly starting to see
That these lies I once believed
Only drag me down
I'm slowly starting to know
That You're the only One
Who will always be there
Even in my dark moments
I want to let You in
I need to let You take my hand
Please open my eyes
To all who You are
And to all that You will have for me

Rescue Me From Death

Help me
I need Your light to shine
To penetrate the dark
That has taken over my soul
To speak truth through the lies
That are destroying my mind
And slowly eating my heart
Save me
Before my world crumbles completely
Before I drown in this loneliness
From the fear that holds me every night
Hear me
As my spirit calls to You
Needing You to listen
To hold me again
And protect me from the enemy
Take me
Back into Your arms
I am calling for You!
Jesus, please rescue me
Before the end comes
Before it's too late

Hidden Scars

How did I get here?
How did I fall
Into the ocean of pain
And this sea of tears
I'm calling to You now
Hoping You'll hear
Needing You to see
All the hurt I hide
And all the unseen scars

In The Darkest Storm

Help me fight
The battle that rages
On the inside
As these demons try
To tear me apart
Help me praise You
Even when the sky
And the storm around me grows dark
Help me to see You
In the small things
And show me Your love
Even when the world
Around me grows cold

Needing Rescue

I need Your rescue
I need Your love
I need Your forgiveness
I need Your strength
To get me out of this hell
That my mind created
I need You to restore me
Revive my spirit
Help me come alive again
Re-ignite the flame
Of this passion I once had for You
I'm crying out once again
For You to be my savior
To reach out to me
And once again hold me in Your arms

Removing What You Hide

I'll look inside your soul
I'll search the deepest parts
I'll cut out the pride
And all the hate that built up
I'll remove all your doubt
And your sorrow that you hide
I'll give you peace and love
That you could never imagine
I'll remove the heart of stone
And replace it with a heart
Of faith and trust
I will help you
If you want me to

Parting Our Ways

This is where it ends
Where we say goodbye
We could have been more
We could have had the world
But now it ends here
And now these tears come
As we part ways
One by one we disappear
Into the darkness of night
Where we fight our own wars
Where we will find our own way
This wasn't the way I thought
That it would have been
But now the nightmares come true
And these dreams all fade
We say we will remember
As we slowly forget
And then say goodbye
And we will walk away
With these distant memories
All too close to our hears

Spiraling

Red alert, red alert!
My walls are closing in
My world is spinning fast
Save me before I crash
I'm calling out, searching
For a hand to grasp

By My Side

Heal this broken heart
Take my life and make it whole
Hold my hand and walk
By my side and if I fall
Catch me and help me to my feet
Restore my hurting soul
And keep me close
Never let me go
Stay with me
And if these tears start to fall
Wipe them away and show me
How much You love me
And that You will always be
By my side